# close friends

# close friends

VICKY CEELEN

**Andrews McMeel Publishing**

Kansas City

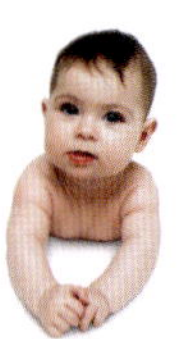

For close friends everywhere,
no matter how far apart,
or how unlikely...

close friends are

"A true friend is someone who thinks you are a good egg even though he knows that you are slightly cracked."

BERNARD MELTZER

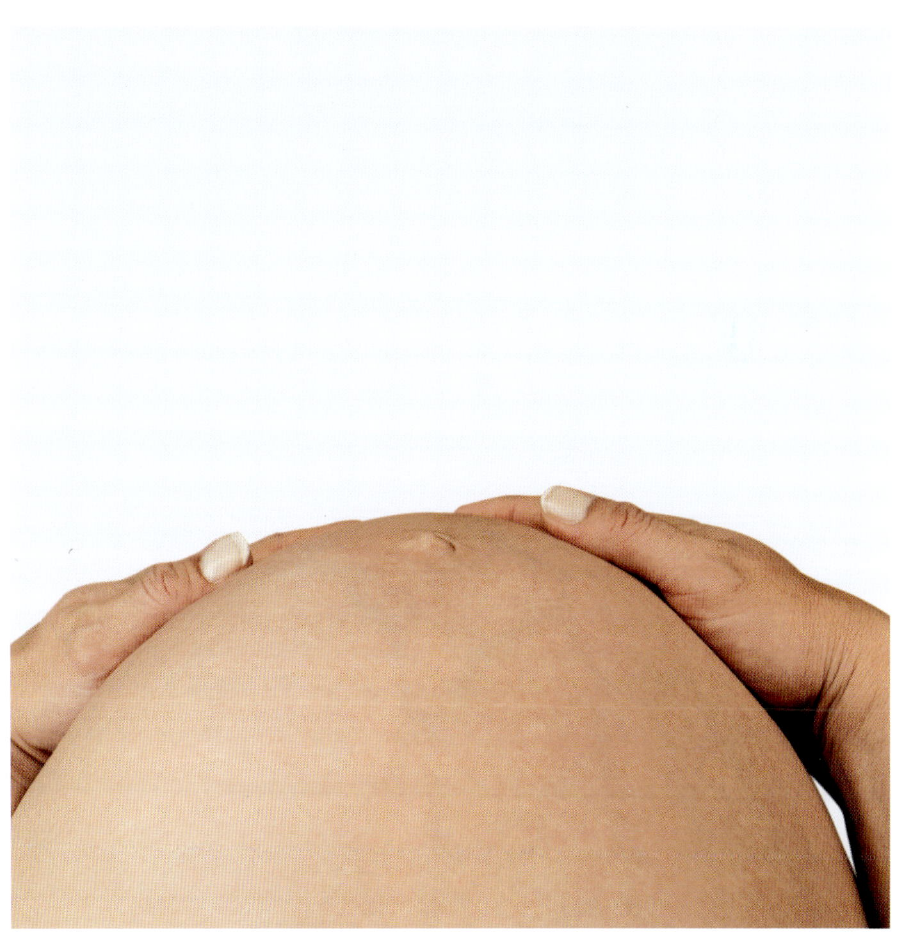

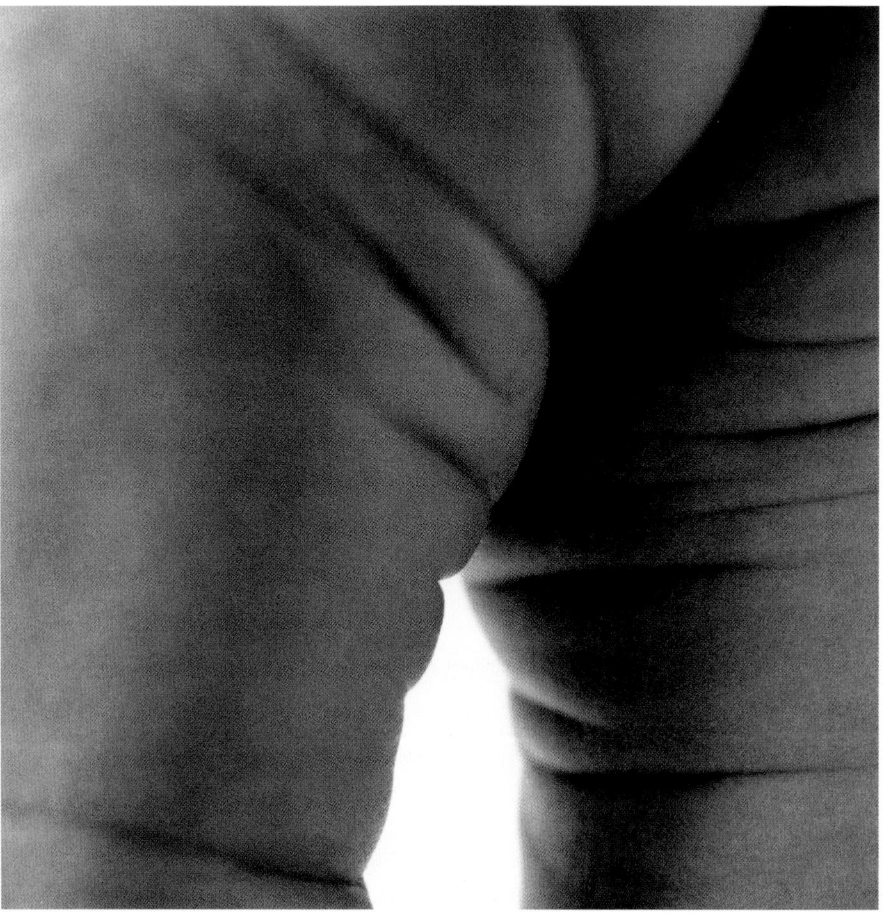

close friends stic

When you're in jail, a friend will be trying to bail you out. A close friend will be in the cell next to you saying, "Damn, that was fun."

ogether

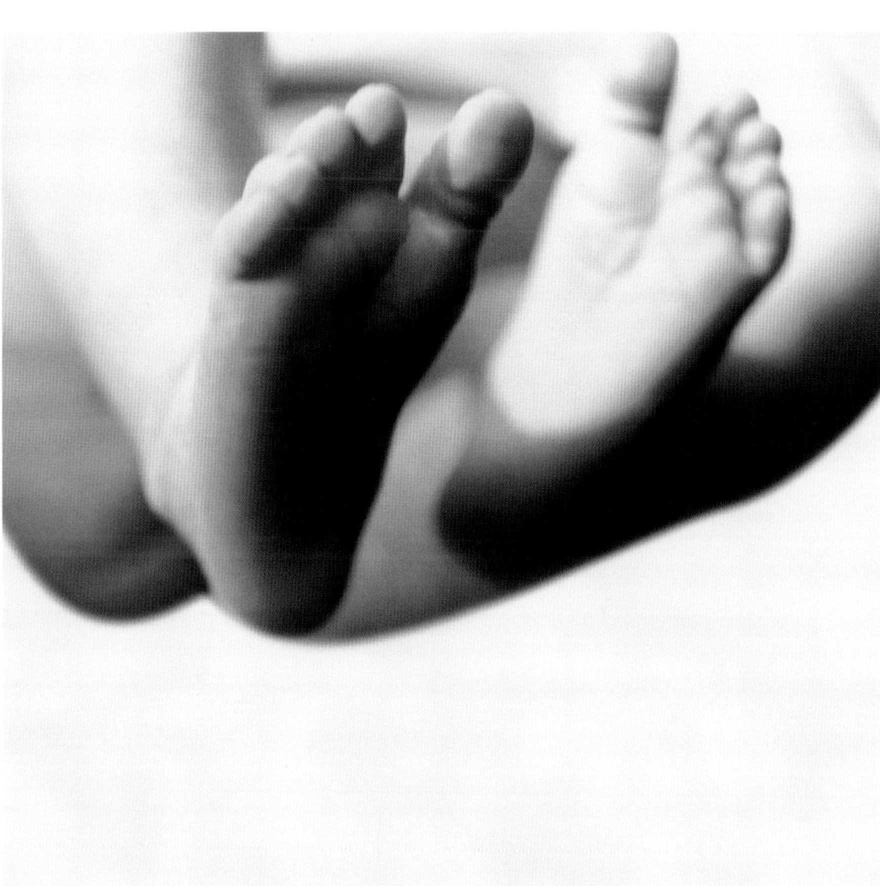

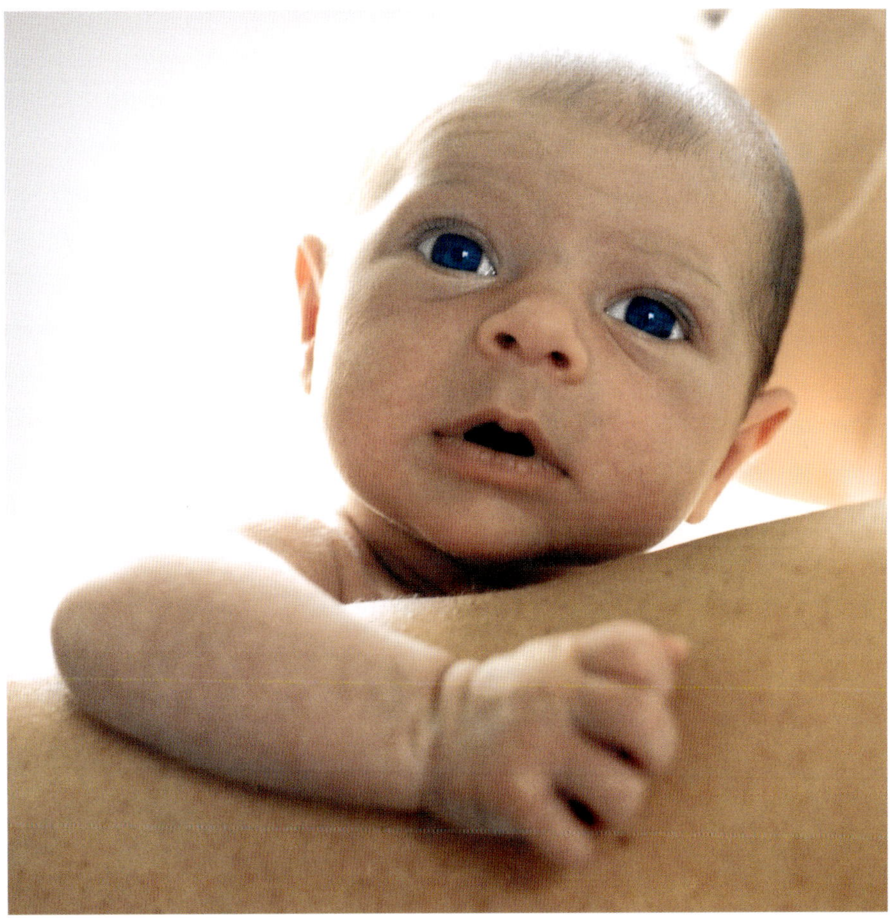

close friends ar

“Friendship is one mind in two bodies.”

MENCIUS

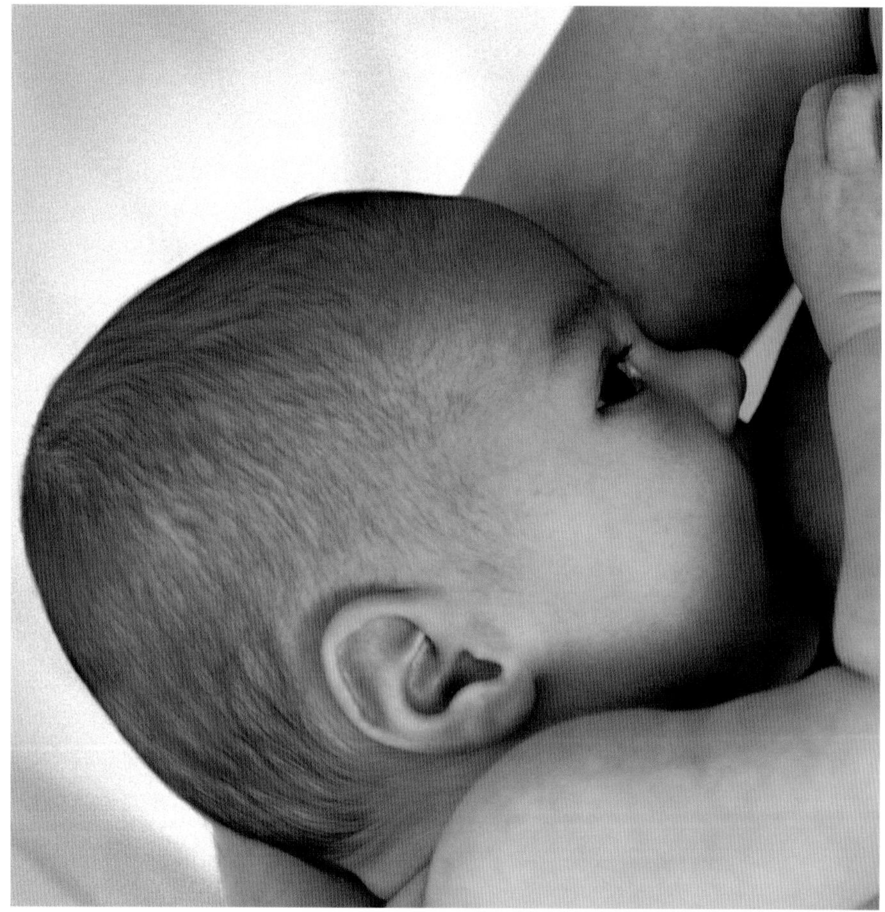

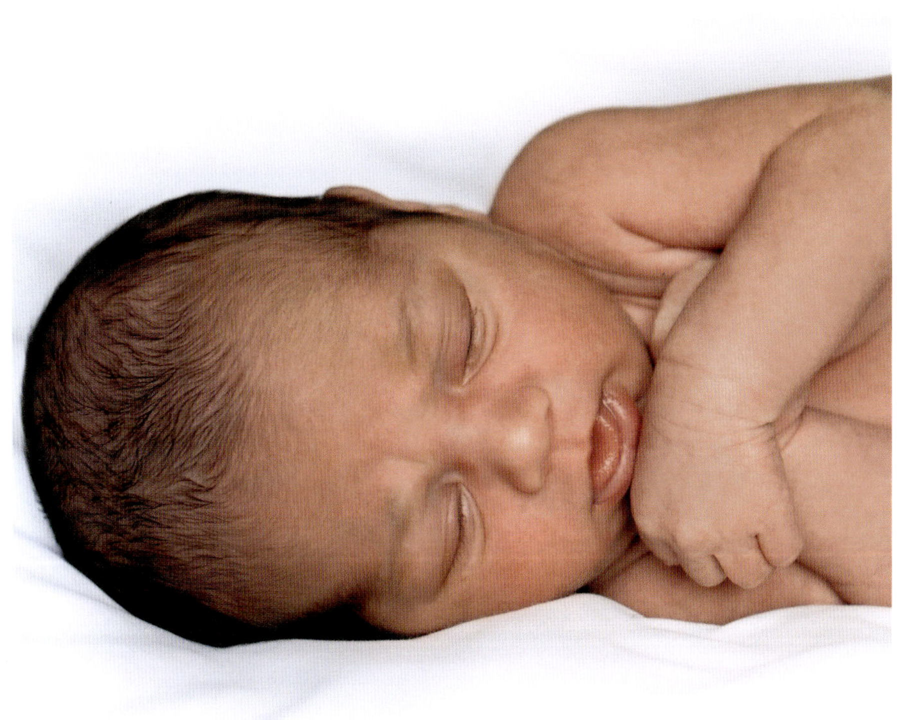

close friends ar

Friends have a way of speaking without words.

thoughtful

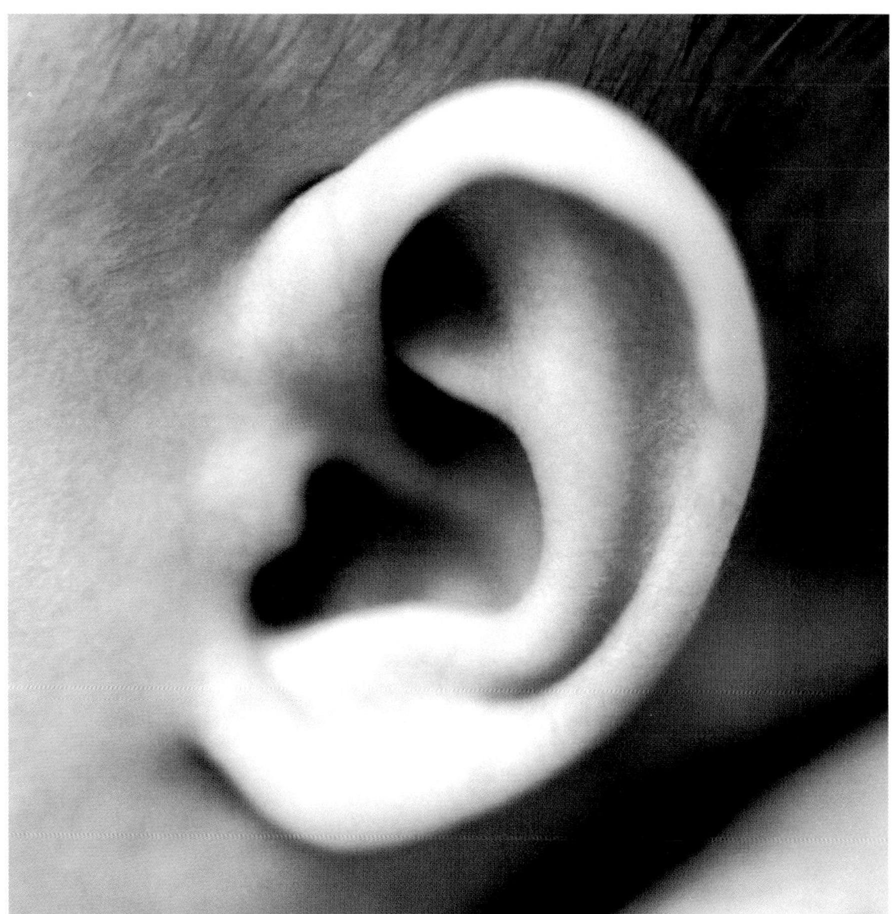

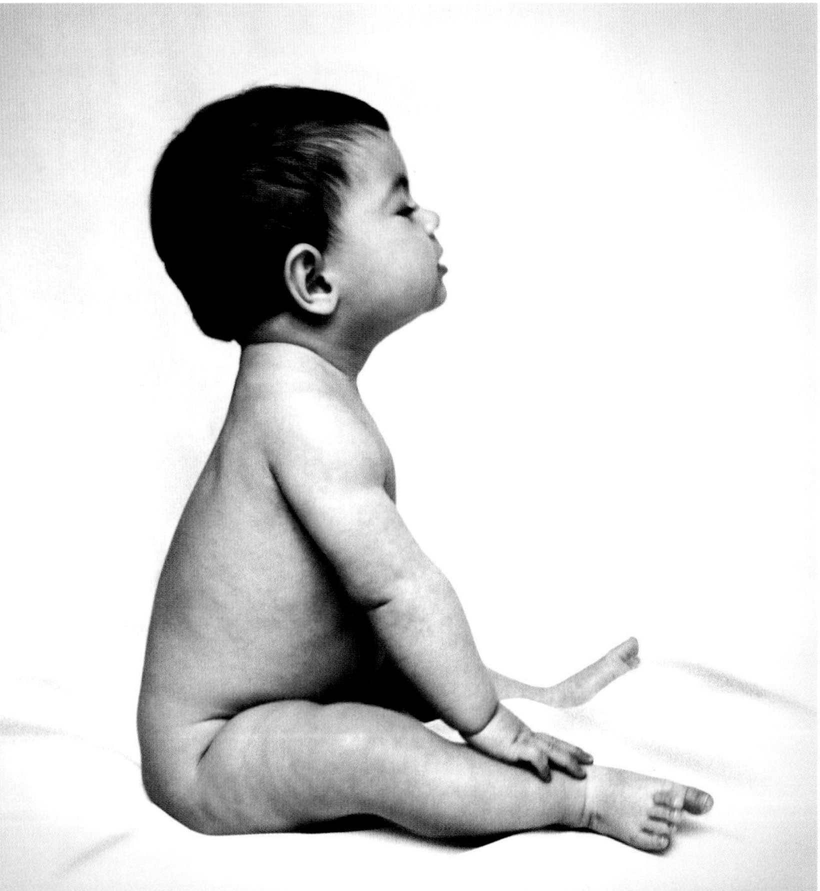

close friends

A friend is somebody you want to be around when you feel like being yourself.

nderstand

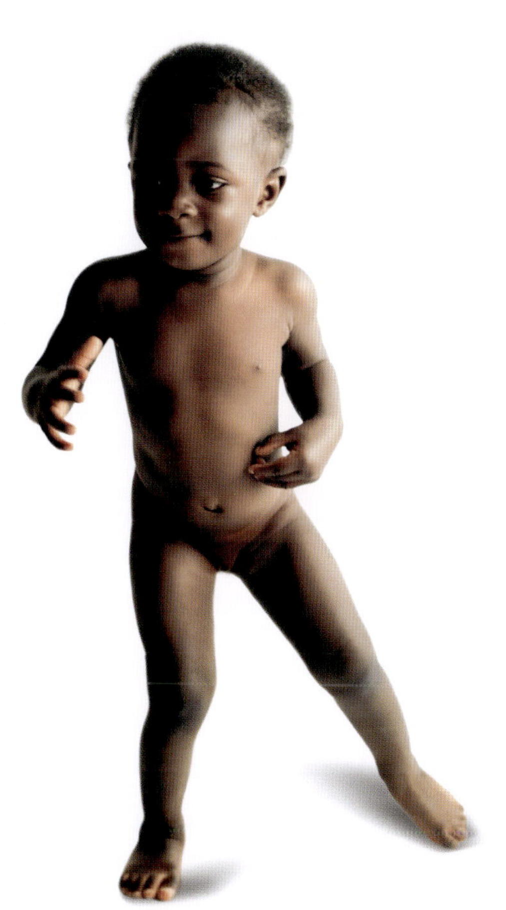

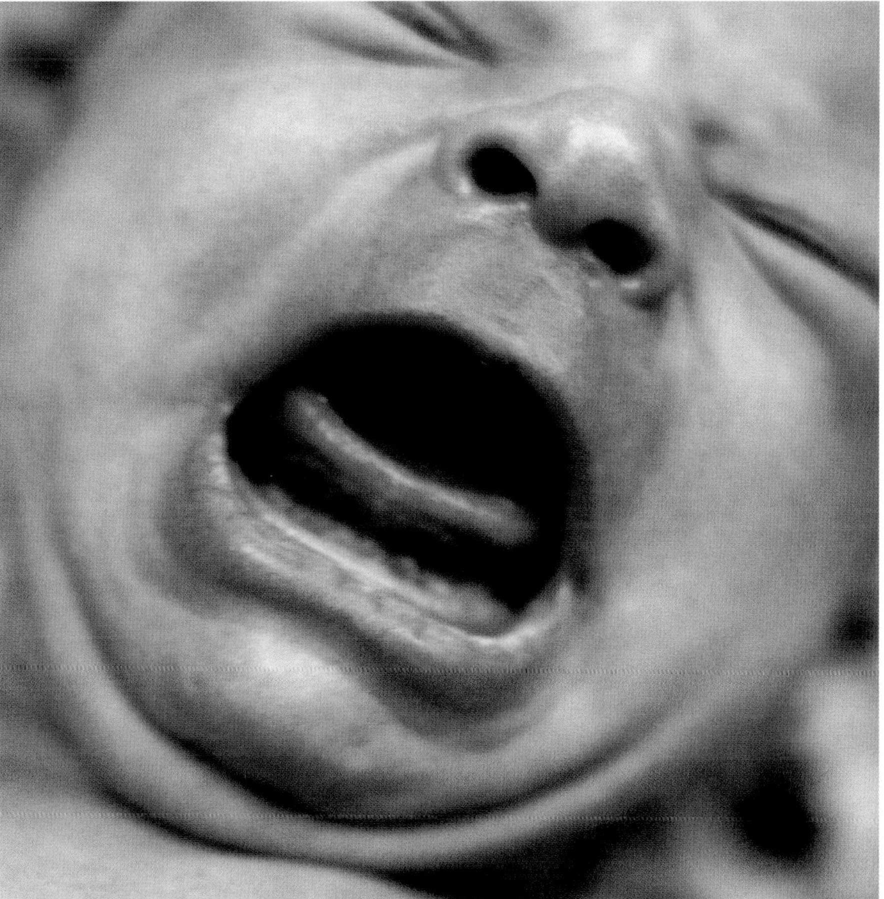

close friends are

"Life is full of people who
will make you laugh, cry, smile
until your face hurts, and so happy that
you think you'll burst.
But the ones who leave their footprints
on your soul are the ones that
keep your life going."

NATALIE BERNOT

soul mates

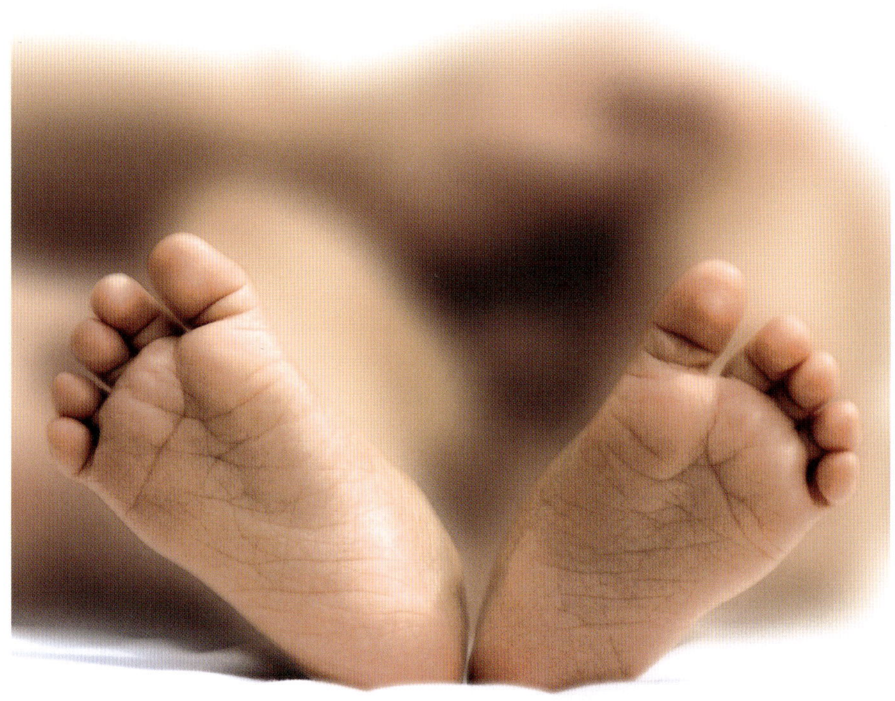

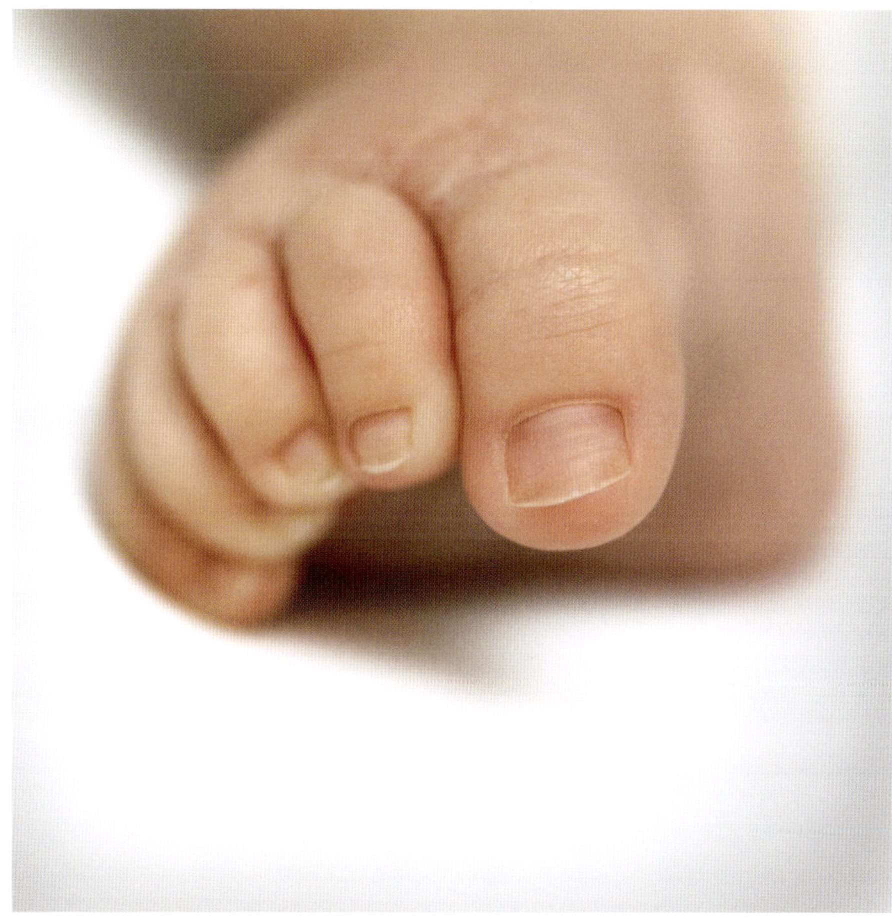

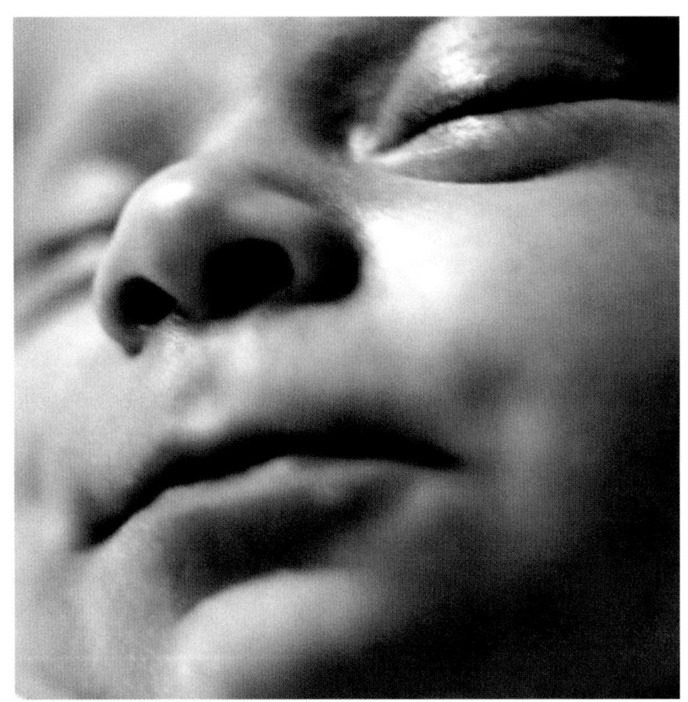

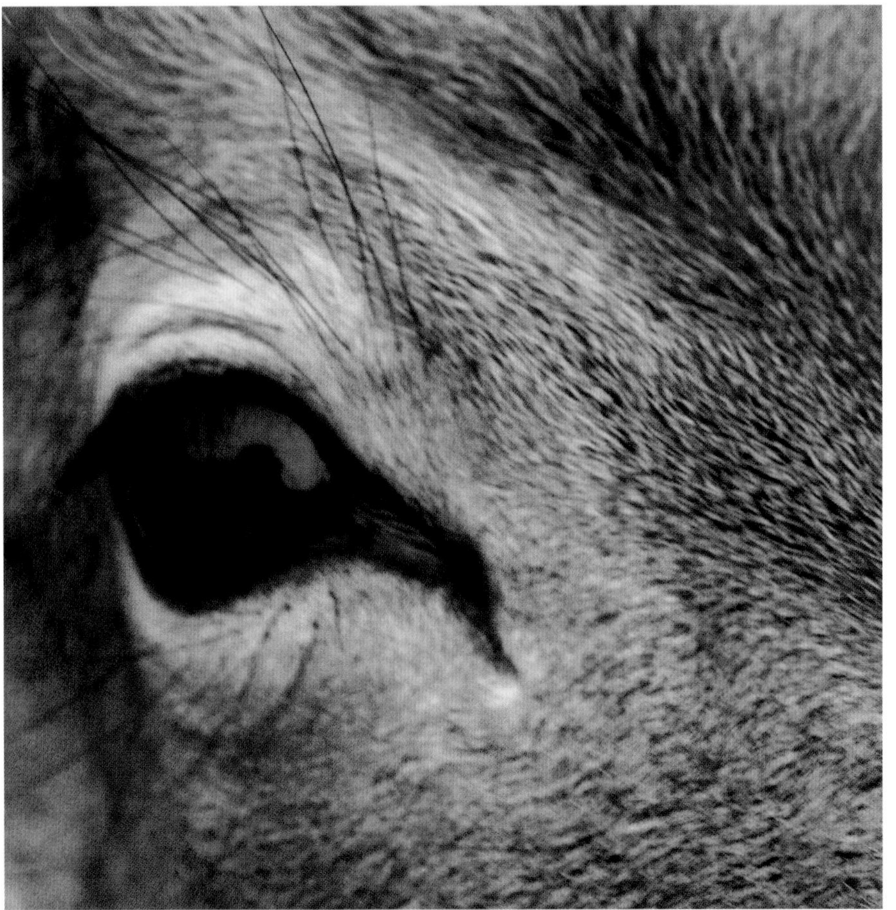

close friends mak

If I could reach up and hold a star
for every time you made me smile,
the entire evening sky would be in
the palm of my hand.

ach other happy

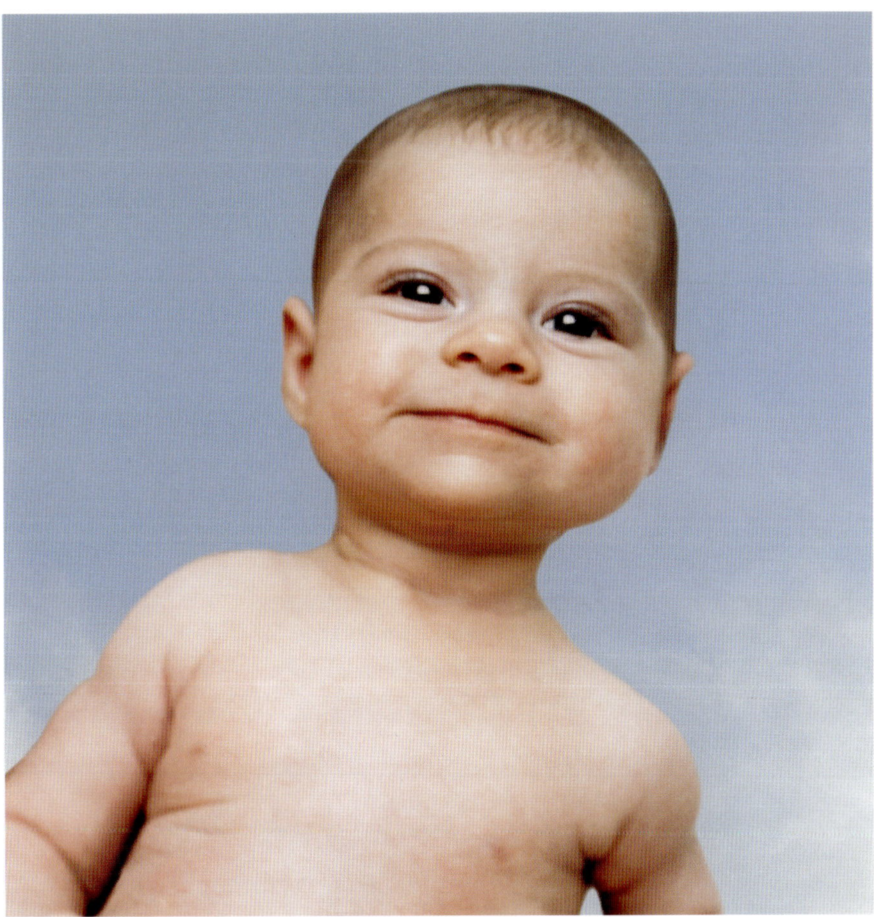

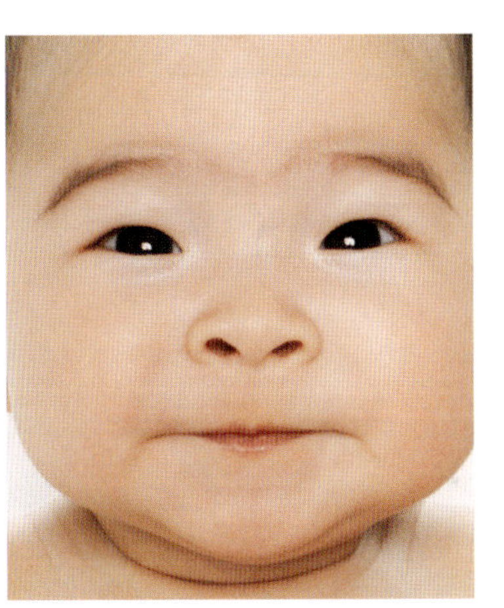

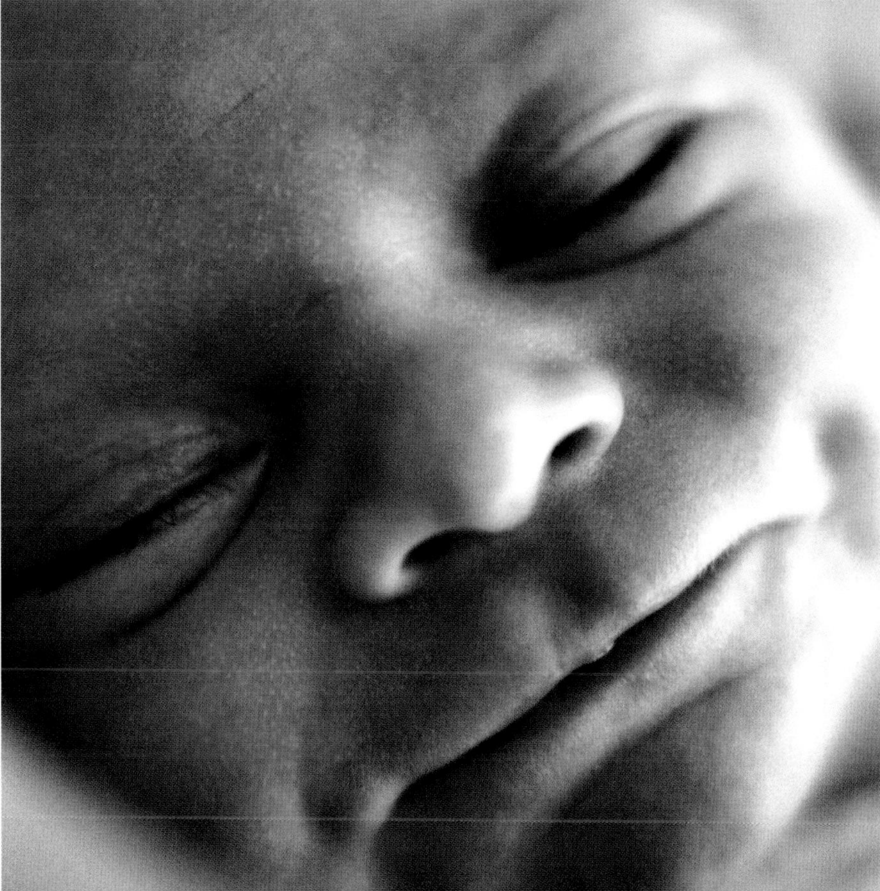

# close friends are forever

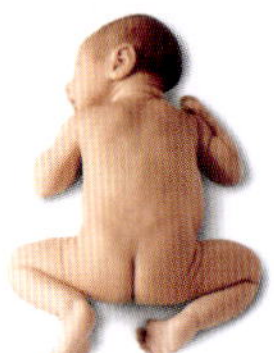

I wish to thank all the babies and their parents. Thanks to Antoine, Dalla, Dramane, Ines (and her mother), Oumon, Ruben and Sophie. Thanks to my agent Veronique Roc, without whom I could not have made this book.

Thanks also to Emeric Dubois, Eliane Girard, Claire Prat-Marca and Joelle Lemaux from the baby-swimmers association Les Mouettes de Paris. For material and logistics, thanks to Jean-Francois Gallois and his team at Central Color; all the images by Vicky Ceelen were shot on Fujicolor film and Fuji Neopan black and white film; thanks to Jean-Philippe Varin at Jacana Wildlife Studios; to Eric Mazarin, Romuald, Benoit, Caroline and Pascal at KeepCoul; Eric Denoulet at Pentax. Thanks to the Chambourcy Animal Centre for permission to photograph the animals featured in this book, to La Vallee des Singes of Romagne, to Doue-la-Fontaine Zoo, Beauval Zoo, Cerza Animal Park, the Touraine Aquarium, Thoiry Park, the OPIE of Guyancourt, the dog-training team of Harvey Ltd and the breeding kennels of Domaine Belle-Rose. And of course thanks to the animals themselves.

Last but not least, thanks to my assistants: Anne, Cindy, Chan, Laure, Stephane. And thanks to everyone else who contributed to the project.

Published in 2002 by PQ Publishing Limited [a member of the Hodder Headline Group], Studio 3.11, Axis Building, 1 Cleveland Road, Parnell, Auckland, New Zealand.

This edition published in the United States, Canada, UK, and Republic of Ireland by Andrews McMeel Publishing, 4520 Main Street, Kansas City, Missouri 64111.



Designed by Francey Young.
Printed by Midas Printing Limited, Hong Kong.

02 03 04 05 06 MPT 10 9 8 7 6 5 4 3 2 1

Library of Congress Control Number: 2002117426